How To Select A Nursing Home For A Loved One

by

Bradley M. Lakin

How to Select a Nursing Home for a Loved One

All rights, including copyright, in the content of this Book are owned or controlled by the author Brad Lakin.

You are not permitted to copy, broadcast, use for commercial purposes, show or play in public, adapt or change in any way the content of this book for any other purpose whatsoever without the prior written permission of the author.

This book was written to provide families with valuable information regarding nursing homes. It is not intended to be "Advertising Material," but the information contained herein may be considered advertising material by some.

The author and publisher do not make any representations or warranties regarding the accuracy of the information contained herein and specifically disclaim all warranties, including without limitation, warranties of fitness for a particular purpose.

Nothing in this book is intended to be legal advice. The author and his firm do not provide legal advice unless there is a written representation agreement. Please understand that your legal matter, if one exists, is unique, different and like no others. Likewise, each jurisdiction has statutes of limitation that impose time limits for when legal claims may be brought. If you need legal advice, you should consult with a qualified attorney about your specific situation and never rely on this book, or any other book for that matter.

Copyright © 2012 Bradley M. Lakin
All rights reserved.
ISBN: 1478344636
ISBN-13: 978-1478344636

Bradley M. Lakin

About the Author

Brad Lakin, Esq. is a best-selling author who has been inducted into *The National Academy of Best Selling Authors* and a trial lawyer who is often sought out by media to discuss his clients' cases. Brad has appeared on ABC, CBS, NBC, FOX affiliates, and CNN, and has been quoted and highlighted in newspapers throughout the country.

Brad has repeatedly been recognized by his peers as a *Super Lawyer*, a *Rising Star*, one of *America's Premier Experts®* and in 2006 as one of *Forty Lawyers Under Forty to Watch*. He has also been honored as a *Top 100 Trial Lawyer* by *The National Trial Lawyers*, a nationwide organization. These honors stem from his success as a litigator in the courtroom.

In a 2005 product liability trial, Lakin helped his clients win a $43 million victory – the second largest verdict in Illinois and the 30th nationwide. The case was featured throughout the country and included an appearance on CNN's Anderson Cooper 360.

Brad has tried cases to verdict in Illinois, Oklahoma, Arkansas, West Virginia, Nebraska, Missouri, and Ohio.

How to Select a Nursing Home for a Loved One

During the course of his career, his firms have represented clients in all 50 states.

Brad's passion for nursing home abuse cases stems from a personal tragedy that happened to a member of his family. Brad's goal in his work and for this book is to prevent the same type of tragedy from happening to others.

Brad is known nationally for his successful courtroom advocacy in personal injury, mass torts, and a variety of complex litigation matters. His firm has recovered over $700 million in verdicts, settlements, and benefits for their clients.

You can learn more about Brad Lakin and his firm by visiting www.GreatInjuryLawyers.com or call (800) 550-2106.

Table of Contents

Chapter 1..….. **Page 8**
Is Your Loved One Ready For a Nursing Home?
What is a Nursing Home?
When is a Nursing Home Right for Your Loved One?

Chapter 2..…..**Page 11**
Finding Potential Facilities
Setting Your Priorities
Locating Facilities
Medicare Government Website
Eldercare Locator
Local and State Sources of Information
Narrowing Down Your Choices

Chapter 3..…….**Page 21**
Visiting Nursing Homes
Your First Visit
Observations
Talk with Residents and their Families
Talk with Staff
Talk with Administrators
Your Second and Third Visits
Other Visits
State Surveys and Complaint Investigations
Surveys
Complaint Investigations

Chapter 4..……...**Page 33**
Preparing for Admission
Talk to Your Loved One
Spend Time at the New Home
Choose Belongings to Take
Women

Men
Admission Day
How Friends and Family can Help
Help Develop and Review Plan of Care
Call and Visit
Going Out
Talk to the Staff
Take Care of Yourself

Appendix A..**Page 44**
Nursing Home Checklists
Nursing Home Checklist
Nursing Home Review Checklist

Appendix B..**Page 55**
Nursing Home Resident Rights
General Goals Of The Law
Quality Of Life
Provision Of Services and Activities
Participation In Home Administration
Access To The Ombudsman Program
Specific Resident Rights
Rights To Self-Determination
Personal And Privacy Rights
Rights Regarding Abuse And Restraints
Rights To Information
Right To Visits
Transfer And Discharge Rights
Protection Of Personal Funds
Protection Against Medicaid Discrimination

Appendix C.. **Page 63**
Resources
Ombudsmen .... **Page 63**

Citizen Groups..**Page 80**

Nursing Home Abuse Hotlines...........................**Page 93**

Appendix D..**Page 103**

Nursing Home Pre-Admission Form
Pre-Admission Form

Chapter 1

Is Your Loved One Ready for a Nursing Home?

Making the decision to move to a nursing home can be difficult and emotional for both you and your loved one. You will want to consider all your choices, including whether a nursing home itself is the best option. Your community may have other choices available, including:

1) Home care
2) Meal programs, such as Meals on Wheels
3) Assisted-living facilities
4) Senior day care, whether through a church community organization or other facility

It is also possible that your loved one may need nursing home care for a short time after an illness or accident, after which one of these alternatives may be your best choice.

What is a Nursing Home?

Nursing homes provide 24-hour care to people who can no longer take care of themselves. Nursing homes provide complete basic services for all residents, including:

1) A furnished room, either a single or double;
2) Meals and snacks, medically planned;
3) Housekeeping and linen service;
4) Personal care, such as bathing;
5) Full-time, onsite medical staff; and
6) Social activities

When is a Nursing Home Right for You or a Loved One?

A nursing home may be the only choice for people who can no longer care for themselves and who cannot be adequately cared for in their homes by family or in the community. Nevertheless, nursing home placement should be a last resort after all other options for the care of your loved one have been exhausted. Most nursing homes are businesses. Return on their investment is as important to them as to any other business. Nursing home residents typically:

1) Have physical, emotional, or mental problems;
2) Can no longer care for their personal needs, such as eating, bathing, using the toilet, moving around, or

taking medications;

3) Wander away if unsupervised; and

4) Need full-time nursing care.

    If a nursing home is not currently the best choice for your family member, use your time now to investigate and choose the best nursing home. Then, you can be secure knowing that you have planned ahead and are prepared.

Chapter 2

Finding Potential Facilities

Once you have decided that a nursing home is the right solution for your loved one, either now or in the near future, it is time to start investigating nursing homes. This chapter helps you locate and begin evaluating nursing homes.

Setting Your Priorities

Before you begin investigating nursing homes, it is best to take some time and think about what is important to you and your loved one in a nursing home facility. Ask yourself the following questions such as:

1) Does your loved one want a single or double room?
2) Does your loved one have a spouse that wishes to stay in the same room?
3) Does your loved one have special medical needs?
4) How much can your loved one afford to spend?
5) What financial assistance may be available?
6) What social activities does your loved one want the nursing home to provide?

How to Select a Nursing Home for a Loved One

7) Does your loved one want to stay in his or her current neighborhood or move to a different area – even a different city or state – to be closer to family and friends?

By taking the time to think through what is important to you and your loved one, you will be able to objectively evaluate the nursing homes you visit.

Locating Facilities

Once you have determined your priorities, your next step will be to locate nursing homes in the area where you or your family member want to live. Numerous resources are available to help you locate nursing homes and begin evaluating your choices.

Medicare.gov Website

The Medicare website is an excellent place to begin comparing nursing homes because it includes the results of each nursing home's latest inspection. What does this mean? Well, state governments oversee the licensing of nursing homes and ensure that they meet MINIMUM quality and performance standards. States typically inspect every nursing home about once a year – or more if the nursing home is performing poorly or has received complaints.

There are more than 150 regulatory standards that nursing homes must meet at all times, covering everything from food storage and preparation to building safety, adequate nursing practices, and procedures to protect residents from physical or mental abuse.

To access inspection information, go to www.medicare.gov and click on Compare Nursing Homes in your Area. From this website, you can choose to compare nursing homes by geography, proximity, or name:

How to Select a Nursing Home for a Loved One

Once you enter your criteria, you will receive a list of all the nursing homes that match. For example, you might have requested all the nursing homes within 10 miles of your zip code. This initial list includes basic information about the home, such as whether it is a non-profit or for-profit organization, and how many beds it has:

Once a list is pulled up, you can click to mark all the nursing homes you are interested in learning more about. You will then see a second list with more detailed information about the homes you selected, such as the number of health deficiencies in their last inspection:

How to Select a Nursing Home for a Loved One

	Your Selected Nursing Homes	
	EUNICE C SMITH NURSING HOME 1251 COLLEGE AVENUE ALTON, IL 62002 (618) 463-7330 Mapping & Directions	**ROSEWOOD CARE CENTER OF ALTON** 3490 HUMBERT ROAD ALTON, IL 62002 (618) 465-2626 Mapping & Directions
Overall Rating	★★ 2 out of 5 stars	★★★★ 4 out of 5 stars
Health Inspections	★★ 2 out of 5 stars	★★★★ 4 out of 5 stars
Nursing Home Staffing	★★★ 3 out of 5 stars	Star Rating not available[1]
Quality Measures	★★★ 3 out of 5 stars	★★★ 3 out of 5 stars
Fire Safety Inspections	1 Fire Safety Deficiencies	0 Fire Safety Deficiencies
Penalties and Denials of Payment Against the Nursing Home	2 Civil Money Penalties 1 Payment Denials	0 Civil Money Penalties 0 Payment Denials
Complaints and Incidents *what is this?*	3 Complaints 0 Incidents	0 Complaints 0 Incidents
Nursing Home Characteristics		
Program Participation	Medicare and Medicaid	Medicare and Medicaid
Number of Certified Beds	48 Certified Beds	78 Certified Beds
Type of Ownership	Non profit - Corporation	For profit - Corporation
Continuing Care Retirement Community	No	No
Resident & Family Councils	Resident & Family Councils	Resident & Family Councils
Located in a Hospital	No	No

From this screen, you can click on the option to view all information about this nursing home. You will then be able to see detailed information about the nursing home, including staffing and the results of its latest inspection.

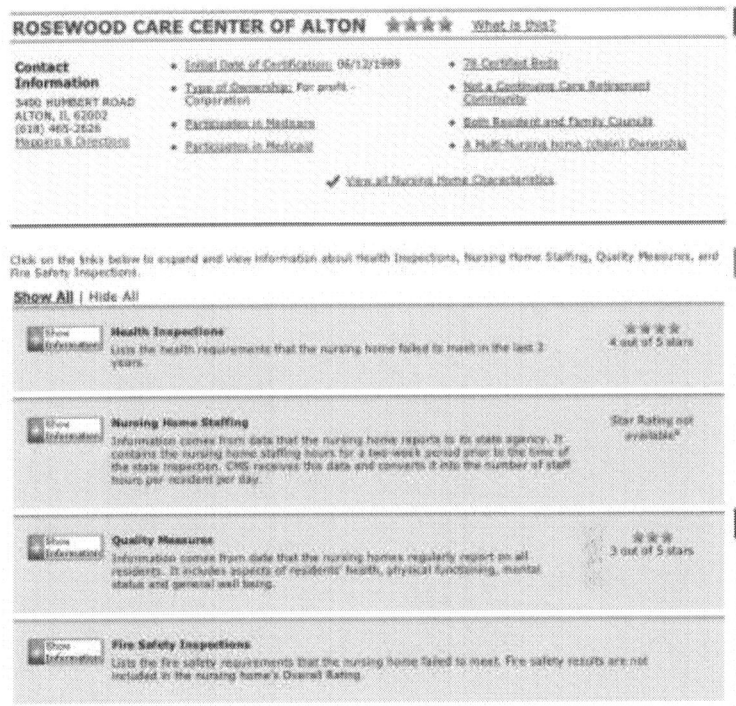

Eldercare Locator

The Eldercare Locator Program helps you find information about state and local area agencies on aging and community-based organizations that serve older adults and their caregivers. You can contact Eldercare Locator by calling 1-800-677-1116 or by going to www.eldercare.gov.

Local and State Sources of Information

Many local and state sources of information are also available:

Ask people you trust (doctors, friends, clergy, neighbors, family, etc.) about their experiences with nursing homes.

Ask your hospital's discharge planner or social worker (Note: some hospitals have referral incentives with nursing homes. So, don't rely on this recommendation alone).

Call your local Administration on Aging or Department of Health. Its number should be in the government section of your phone book, or for a nationwide listing you can visit: www.aoa.gov/eldfam/How_To_Find/Agencies/Agencies.asp.

Contact Your State's Long-Term Care Ombudsman.

Go to www.ltcombudsman.org/static_pages/help.cfm and click on your state to get contact information for your ombudsman. Ombudsmen regularly visit nursing homes and interact with the residents to make sure their rights are being protected. You can ask them about complaints that have been made about particular nursing homes and how the complaints were addressed.

Contact your state's Citizen Advocacy Group, if one is available. Advocacy groups are concerned citizens who work to improve the quality of care for nursing home residents in their area. Go to: www.nursinghomeaction.org/static_pages/citizens_groups.cfm and click on your state to find out whether an advocacy group is available.

Narrowing Down Your Choices

Once you have identified a list of possible nursing homes in your area, it's time to start narrowing down your choices. Begin by calling the nursing homes on your list

How to Select a Nursing Home for a Loved One

and asking preliminary questions such as:

1) Whether it has Medicaid certified beds?
2) What the waiting period is for a bed?
3) Whether it is equipped for patients with your loved one's health conditions (*e.g.*, many nursing homes have specific wings for Alzheimer's patients)?
4) Any other questions specific to your situation. (*e.g.*, whether a married couple can be in the same room together, whether pets are permitted, or how much space is available for personal belongings)?

These questions will help you narrow down your list to the few nursing homes that best meet your requirements. Many nursing homes also have web sites. These are another source of information to help you narrow your list. Once you have identified the nursing homes you are most interested in, you are ready for the next step: personal visits.

Chapter 3

Visiting Nursing Homes

By now, you have narrowed down your nursing home choices to the homes you want to visit. This chapter will help you understand when to visit these nursing homes, what to look for during your visits, and what questions to ask about the facility.

Before you visit any nursing homes, print out the Nursing Home Checklist in Appendix A to serve as a guide for your visits. Take a friend or family member with you to help you remember details.

Your First Visit

You should plan on at least two visits to each nursing home. During your visits, remember that the best-looking nursing home is not always the best choice for your loved one. Yes, you want a facility that is clean and sanitary, but you do not want one that sacrifices resident care and additional staff for new paint and carpet in the lobby.

How to Select a Nursing Home for a Loved One

Call to schedule your first visit, and try to visit during the day – preferably during the late morning and over the lunch hour. This allows you to see residents when they are out of bed and going about their daily routines. It also lets you see the quality of the food and the care provided to residents during mealtime. Pay particular attention to the number of staff members in the dining room. The lack of staff in the dining room often indicates an understaffing problem.

When you arrive at the nursing home, the first thing you should do is ask to see the facility survey, complaint notebook, and the results of its most recent state survey. Pay particular attention to the nursing home personnel's reaction to your request. By law, the nursing home must make these items available to you upon request. If it doesn't have the survey and complaint book available, cross the home off your list and move on.

Check the survey report to see whether the home was cited for deficient practices in any quality-of-care areas. Write down the dates of the surveys for use when you get home to continue your evaluation. Make sure the binder includes all the complaint investigations that exist. If not, it may indicate the nursing home is trying to hide something.

In addition to taking a formal tour of the nursing home, use this visit to make observations and to talk with residents, family, staff members, and administrators.

Observations

Observe how staff members interact with residents. Are they friendly and respectful? Are residents' requests dealt with promptly? Are staff members patient with residents who need help with basic needs such as eating and using the bathroom?

Observe how administrators interact with both staff members and residents. Does everyone seem to get along?

Observe the residents. Do they seem alert and peaceful? Do they look clean, well-groomed, well-fed, and healthy? Do you see any bruises or other physical warning signs? What activities are they participating in?

Observe residents' rooms. Are they clean and do they

How to Select a Nursing Home for a Loved One

reflect the individuality of their occupants?

Observe the residents at mealtime. Do the meals look appetizing? Are residents eating most of their food? Are staff members feeding residents who need help?

Observe common areas. Are the hallways, common rooms, dining rooms, etc. clean? How does the home smell?

Observe call lights in the hallway. How many lights are illuminated at once? How long does it take someone to respond to a call light? (Note: Failure to respond quickly can be an indication that the facility is understaffed)

Talk with residents and their families:
1) Ask residents what they like and don't like about the home.

2) Ask residents' families about any concerns or problems they've had with the home And how their concerns were addressed.

3) Ask residents about their schedules for bedtime, baths,

and meals and whether they are flexible enough to meet the residents' needs.

4) Is the staff responsive to resident requests? Do personnel help the resident with toileting, bathing, eating, etc.?

5) Are healthy snacks, such as fresh fruits and vegetables, available?

6) Ask about security. Does the resident feel safe? Have any of the resident's possessions disappeared?

7) Does the resident get outside for fresh air or activities as much as he or she wants?

8) Are private areas available if residents and their families wish to spend time alone together?

MOST IMPORTANT QUESTION: If you were making the decision today, would you hesitate to put your loved one in this facility?

Talk With Staff

> 1) Ask about the security system. (*e.g.*, What procedures are in place to keep residents safe and secure?);
> 2) If you see any residents in physical restraints, ask why. (*e.g.*, What policies govern the use of restraints?);

How to Select a Nursing Home for a Loved One

3) Ask what activities are available for residents. (*e.g.*, Does the nursing home provide transportation to stores, community activities, or other events?);
4) Ask whether staff members are permanently assigned to residents.
5) Ask what kind of training the staff receives.

Talk With Administrators

1) Ask whether the home has changed ownership or management in the last couple of years. (*e.g.*, How long have the current Administrator and Director of Nursing been at the home?);
2) Ask about staff turnover. (*e.g.*, How long do staff members usually stay at their jobs? How does the administration encourage staff retention?);
3) Ask how the administration encourages resident and family input and ideas for improving the nursing home. (*e.g.*, Is there a resident and/or a family council?);
4) Ask about the nursing home staff. (*e.g.*, Is there a social worker, a physical therapist, and an activities director? Which physicians visit regularly or are on call?

5) Ask how they find competent staff. (*e.g.*, Do they advertise for staff? Are they currently advertising for staff members, and if so, what type? What is their toughest challenge in staffing? Have they ever requested additional staff members and been denied?)

Your Second and Third Visits

Your first visit to the nursing home was a formal, scheduled meeting. You will want to make at least one, if not two, additional UNANNOUNCED visits. Just simply show up and say you're considering the facility and haven't been able to make it during the day because of work or other conflicts. Make these visits on a weekend or evening so you can see how the staffing differs from your previous visit.

You should go once on a weekend at or near the shift change and once during the evening just before visiting hours end, or after visiting hours if possible. Shifts in nursing homes are typically 7 am-3 pm, 3 pm -11 pm, and 11 pm-7 am. The best time to evaluate whether the nursing home has sufficient staff is when it does not expect visitors to be present. Spend 15 minutes or more in the dining room for those who need assistance during the evening meal.

Ask a resident for permission to visit at their table. Sit and observe the care of the most frail residents during this lower staffing time. This may be the best way to see the heart of the nursing home, especially if the visit is on the weekend

Other Visits

If possible, arrange to attend a resident or resident council meeting. This will give you insight into any issues facing the nursing home, as well as let you see the communication process between administrators and residents/families. Request the names and phone numbers of three members of the resident council. Call them and discuss the nursing home. Ask if they were choosing a nursing home today would they hesitate to put their loved one in this particular nursing home. If there is any hesitation, you should probably move on to another home unless it has an otherwise favorable history.

State Surveys and Complaint Investigations

State agencies perform two types of reviews of nursing home facilities:

1) Surveys
2) Complaint Investigations

Surveys are conducted annually each 12 or 15 months. Complaint investigations are specifically conducted after the agency receives a complaint about a home. Usually a complaint investigation is conducted within 30 days unless there is actual harm to residents, in which case it can happen within 24 hours.

State surveys should be used as red flags to stay away from bad facilities, not for choosing a good facility. Stay away from facilities with many citations, but do not assume that those without many citations are good. Why? Because all too often facilities are undercited. Citations are discouraged by the central offices of the licensing agencies.

More citations mean more work and expense for the state licensing agency since the nursing homes almost routinely appeal the findings against them and keep the agency attorneys tied up in hearings for many months and even years. It is an accepted fact that nursing homes are pre-notified of pending inspections as noted from the flurry of activity preceding inspections. A large percentage of inspectors are ex nursing home nurses and administrators who are friendly to this industry, according to *"Patients Pain and Politics,"* a personal account by nurse inspector, Mary Richards Rollins.

Surveys

Although surveys and complaint investigations provide valuable information, remember that it is common for a home to be cited for some deficiencies in its annual state survey. Your concern should be whether the home is routinely cited for the same deficiency year after year. This indicates that the home is not taking steps to correct the problem.

To check older surveys to see whether the same deficiencies routinely appear, look for the *"f-tags."* These are codes associated with each deficiency: for example, F357. Pay particular attention to the scope and severity of the deficiency. This information is usually found right under the "*f-tags*" and will say "*ss=_*." The chart will help you determine the scope and severity of the deficiency:

	Isolated	Patterned	Widespread
Immediate Jeopardy	J	K	L
Actual Harm	G	H	I
Potential for Harm	D	E	F
No Harm	A	B	C

Pay close attention to any deficiency with a severity and scope of D, E, F, G, H, I, J, K, or L.

Complaint Investigations

Complaint investigation reports should be available at the nursing home, or your ombudsmen can help you get this information.
(www.ltcombudsman.org/static_pages/help.cfm)

Complaint investigations should be BIG RED FLAGS. This is not to say that nursing homes that provide quality care do not have complaint investigations. You need to read the investigation file and determine the severity of the complaint and the state's findings (as described in the previous section). Although this may seem like a lot of work, it is probably the most vital aspect of

How to Select a Nursing Home for a Loved One

choosing a nursing home.

As you read complaint investigations, pay particular attention to issues such as:

Bedsores
Infections
Falls
Malnutrition
Dehydration
Failure to medicate
Failure to monitor
Assault
Staffing
Failure to conduct background checks on employees
    Citations for these issues should be seriously considered as you evaluate nursing homes.

Chapter 4

Preparing for Admission

You have analyzed a variety of nursing homes, visited several, and finally chosen the one that is best for your family member. Now it is time to prepare for admission.

Being admitted to a nursing home is stressful for both the new resident and for family members. The new resident deals with worries about loss of freedom and independence, as well as the physical loss of cherished belongings that must be sold, stored, or given away. He or she may even feel angry and bitter. Family members, on the other hand, often feel guilty that they cannot properly care of their loved one.

So how can you ease the transition to a nursing home and make it easier for everyone? This chapter gives you some ideas to help you make a happy and healthy adjustment to the new home.

Talk WITH Your Loved One

How to Select a Nursing Home for a Loved One

As stated earlier, moving to a nursing home is stressful for everyone. It is important to talk openly with each other about your fears, doubts, and concerns. At the same time though, think of the many positive aspects the change will bring about:

1) Less worry about medical and physical needs;
2) Help with basic needs, such as keeping track of medication;
3) New opportunities for social interaction; and
4) No worries about home repair and maintenance.

Spend Time at the New Home

Before your loved one actually moves into the nursing home, he or she should spend some time there getting comfortable. Attend social activities, have a few meals, meet with the social worker or recreation director, and get to know other residents, especially a future roommate.

Also, see whether you can take care of any admission paperwork in advance, to make the admission day easier. Use the form in Appendix D to identify current medical conditions, the reason/s for nursing home admission, and a list of medications. You should provide this to the nursing home personnel upon admission and keep a copy for your records.

Choose Belongings to Take

As part of your visit to the home you selected, you should have learned how much space your loved one will have for personal belongings. Begin going through possessions to choose the items you want to take to personalize your loved one's room. Include family photos, books, quilts or blankets, pillows, mementos, possibly even a favorite chair if the nursing home allows personal furniture.

Use this time to share memories and stories with family and friends. This is also a good time for loved ones to pass on family heirlooms and other cherished possessions.

In addition to personal belongings, you need to think about what clothes to take. ElderCare Online (www.ec-online.net) suggests the following items:

<u>**Women**</u>

How to Select a Nursing Home for a Loved One

Clothing:

5-8 dresses (back-snap dresses if incontinent)
5-8 changes of underwear
6 pairs of socks or stockings
2 pairs of slippers

2 pairs of shoes
3-6 pairs of pajamas or gowns
2 robes
3 sweaters
Coat and hat/scarf

Personal Care Items:

Toothbrush
Deodorant
Body lotion
Powder
Shampoo
Hairpins and rollers (if used)
Brush and comb
Make-up/cosmetics (if used)
Writing materials
Small standing cosmetic mirror for table

Men

Clothing:

5-8 pants/shirts
5-8 changes of underwear
2 pairs of shoes
8 pairs of socks
2 pairs of slippers

3-6 pairs of pajamas
2 robes
3 sweaters
Coat and hat/scarf

Personal Care Items:

Toothbrush
Deodorant
Body lotion
Powder
Shampoo
Shaving equipment
Brush and comb
Writing materials

Clothes should be machine wash and dry and not need ironing. Also, be sure to label all clothing and other personal belongings.

Admission Day

It is a self-serving practice of many hospitals to transfer patients to nursing homes on a Friday. Because nursing home staffing is at its worse on weekends, residents can have a very difficult time adjusting. To avoid transfer trauma and ensure a smooth beginning, plan to admit early in the week.

How to Select a Nursing Home for a Loved One

On your loved one's first day at the nursing home, a friend or family member should go along to help set up the room, meet staff members and other residents, and explore the new facilities. Find out whether the home has a welcoming committee to help your loved one meet people and adjust to the new routine.

Before family and visitors leave, try to get your loved one involved in an activity so he or she won't be so lonely when left alone. Also, if he or she wanders or has dementia, make sure he or she is wearing a wanderguard bracelet before you leave. This is an alarm device that alerts staff if and when your loved one ever tries to walk out of the home.

How Friends and Family can Help

Your loved one may feel lonely and sad after entering a nursing home, especially for the first two or three weeks. You can help make their transition easier with the following tips:

Help Develop and Review the Plan of Care

Nursing homes must develop a plan of care for all residents, which outlines how staff will care for each resident. It clearly states what each staff member will do and when it will happen.

For example, your loved one's plan of care might include assistance with walking a certain distance each day to build strength and maintain muscle.

Care plans can address both medical and non-medical issues. For example, incompatibility with a roommate could be addressed in the regular plan-of-care meeting.

For care plans to work, residents must feel comfortable with them and agree they meet their needs. You can help develop the initial plan of care based on your knowledge of your loved one's needs, likes, and dislikes.

Care plans must be reviewed and revised regularly. Care plan meetings are required by federal law at least every quarter, but can be requested by the family at any time if there is a change in condition such as persistent weight loss, development of bedsores, or depression.

How to Select a Nursing Home for a Loved One

The plan of care must be a formal agreement between representatives from all disciplines, including dietary, social services, nursing, physical therapy, direct care givers and the administrator.

Make it known before the meeting begins that you would like to have a hard copy of the written plan of care, and then be sure you receive one at the end of your meeting. This is the time to be specific about the resident's needs and discuss them in detail. If there is weight loss for example, ask that a specific snack be given at specific times, such as 10 am and 3 pm, or an extra serving of his favorite food is provided at breakfast when he is most hungry. This way you can check to be sure that the changes have been made.

A violation of the plan of care can carry a $10,000 fine. The family must be notified of the plan of care meeting and should make every effort to attend. If it is scheduled for an inconvenient time, ask that it be rescheduled.

Call and Visit

Encourage out-of-town friends and family members to call and send letters. Call and visit as often as possible, but keep your visits fairly short: 15 to 30 minutes is a good amount of time, at least in the beginning when your loved one is still adjusting to his or her new environment.

During your visit, plan to share an activity, such as a manicure, eating a snack or meal together, looking at photos or listening to music. When it's time to leave, have the staff engage your loved one in a new activity.

Going Out

Once your loved one seems to be adjusting and his or her health permits, go out together for a day of shopping or a new movie – whatever activity you have always enjoyed together. If you make plans together, make every effort to keep them or your loved one will be disappointed.

Talk to the Staff

If you are concerned about your loved one's

adjustment to the nursing home, talk to the staff, especially the social worker. The staff will be able to give you advice to help him or her adjust. You can also help the staff get to know your loved one by sharing details about his or her likes, dislikes and daily routines.

Take Care of Yourself

You also need to consider your own feelings. If you had been caring for your loved one, you may be feeling both guilt and relief – even guilty that you feel relieved!

When you begin to feel overwhelmed by guilt, remind yourself why a nursing home is the best option for your loved one. Accept the fact that sometimes people need more care than one person can provide – even a loving, dedicated person such as you.

It also helps to talk to friends and other people who have been through this same situation. Find out whether a support group is available, either through the nursing home itself or elsewhere in your community.

Remember, you too are going through a transition and your feelings are perfectly normal. However, you need to work through your feelings so you can support your loved one and help make his or her adjustment easier.

How to Select a Nursing Home for a Loved One

Appendix A

NURSING HOME CHECKLIST (adapted from www.medicare.gov)			
Name of Nursing Home: _____ Date of Visit:_____			
Basic Information			
QUESTIONS	Yes	No	Comments
The nursing home is Medicare-certified.			
The nursing home is Medicaid-certified.			
The nursing home has the level of care needed (e.g. skilled, custodial), and a bed is available.			
The nursing home has special services if needed in a separate unit (e.g. dementia, ventilator, or rehabilitation), and a bed is available.			
The nursing home is located close enough for friends and family to visit.			

Resident Appearance

QUESTIONS	Yes	No	Comments
Residents are clean, appropriately dressed for the season or time of day, and well groomed.			
Residents appear healthy and happy.			

Nursing Home Living Spaces

QUESTIONS	Yes	No	Comments
The nursing home is free from overwhelming unpleasant odors.			
The nursing home appears clean and well kept.			
The temperature in the nursing home is comfortable for residents.			
The nursing home has good lighting.			
Noise levels in the dining room and other common areas are comfortable.			
Smoking is not allowed or may be restricted to certain areas of the nursing home.			
Furnishings are sturdy, yet comfortable and attractive.	.		

Staff

QUESTIONS	Yes	No	Comments
The relationship between the staff and the residents appears to be warm, polite, and respectful.			
All staff members wear nametags.			
Staff members knock on the door before entering a resident's room and refer to residents by name.			
The nursing home offers a training and continuing education program for all staff.			
The nursing home does background checks on all staff.			
The guide on your tour knows the residents by name and is recognized by them.			
The home has a full-time Registered Nurse (RN) present all times, other than the Administrator or Director of Nursing.			
The same team of nurses and Certified Nursing Assistants (CNAs) work with the same resident 4 to 5 days per week.			
CNAs work with a reasonable number of residents.			
CNAs are involved in care			

planning meetings.			
The staff includes a full-time social worker.			
The staff has a licensed doctor. Is he or she there daily? Can he or she be reached at all times?			
The nursing home's management team has worked together for at least one year.			
Key staff members work full-time rather than part-time.			
There is an adequate ratio of nurses and certified nursing assistants per number of residents.			

Residents' Rooms

QUESTIONS	Yes	No	Comments
Residents may have personal belongings and/or furniture in their rooms.			
The home has safety features such as railings and grab bars in residents' rooms and bathrooms.			
Each resident has storage space (closet and drawers) in his or her room.			
Each bedroom has a window.			
Residents have access to a personal telephone and television.			

How to Select a Nursing Home for a Loved One

Residents have a choice of roommates.			
Residents can reach water pitchers.			
The home has policies and procedures to protect a resident's possessions.			

Hallways, Stairs, Lounges, and Bathrooms

QUESTIONS	Yes	No	Comments
Exits are clearly marked.			
There are quiet areas where residents can visit with friends and family.			
The nursing home has smoke detectors and sprinklers.			
All common areas, resident rooms, and doorways are designed for wheelchair use.			
The home has handrails in the hallways and grab bars in the bathrooms.			
Hallways are kept clear of obstructions such as housekeeping carts.			

Menus and Food

QUESTIONS	Yes	No	Comments
Residents have a choice of food			

items at each meal. (Ask whether favorite foods are served.)			
Nutritious snacks are served twice daily			
Staff help residents eat and drink at mealtimes if help is needed.			

Activities

QUESTIONS	Yes	No	Comments
Residents, including those who are unable to leave their rooms, may choose to take part in a variety of activities.			
The home offers a variety of activities for residents to choose from.			
The nursing home has outdoor areas for resident use, and staff members help residents go outside.			
The nursing home has an active volunteer program.			

Safety and Care

QUESTIONS	Yes	No	Comments
The nursing home has an emergency evacuation plan and conducts regular fire drills.			
Residents get preventive care, such as a yearly flu shot, to help keep them healthy.			

How to Select a Nursing Home for a Loved One

Residents may still see their personal doctors.			
The nursing home has an arrangement with a nearby hospital for emergencies.			
Care plan meetings are scheduled at times that are convenient for residents and family members to attend whenever possible.			
The nursing home has corrected all deficiencies (failure to meet one or more federal or state requirements) on its last state inspection report, or has a plan in place to correct these deficiencies.			
The building includes fire extinguishers, smoke detectors, carbon monoxide detectors, and a sprinkler system.			
The home has emergency plans to deal with natural disasters.			

State Surveys and Complaint History

QUESTIONS	Yes	No	Comments
A survey and complaint notebook is available. (note dates of surveys and complaint investigation for future)			
The home has a history of deficiencies.			

The home has a history of complaints that have been investigated by the state.			
Any of the complaints or deficiencies involve: Bedsores Infections Falls Malnutrition Dehydration Failure to medicate Failure to monitor Assault Staffing Failure to conduct background checks on employees			
The nursing home has corrected all deficiencies (failure to meet one or more federal or state requirements) on its last state inspection report, or a plan is in place to correct these deficiencies.			

Additional Comments:

How to Select a Nursing Home for a Loved One

NURSING HOME REVIEW CHECKLIST

Resident or Family Council

QUESTIONS	Yes	No	Comments
The nursing home has a Resident or Family Council that meets regularly.			
Staff and administration are open to suggestions and ideas developed by the Resident or Family Council.			

Plan of Care

QUESTIONS	Yes	No	Comments
The staff is following the Plan of Care.			
The Plan of Care is reviewed regularly to make necessary adjustments.			
The resident or family feels included in Plan of Care process.			

Monitor the Facility

QUESTIONS	Yes	No	Comments
The nursing home continues to feel safe, clean, and comfortable.			
Staff members are caring			

My loved one receiving care/attention.			
Staff and Communication			
QUESTIONS	Yes	No	Comments
Staff members are willing to talk to me about my loved one's care			
Staff members keep me informed about any changes in my loved one's health, behavior, eating habits, etc.			
Inspections			
QUESTIONS	Yes	No	Comments
I have reviewed the latest nursing home inspection report.			
The nursing home is correcting all deficiencies (failure to meet one or more federal or state requirements) on its last state inspection report, or has a plan to correct these deficiencies.			
Monitor the Local Paper			
QUESTIONS	Yes	No	Comments
The nursing home advertises for new staff members frequently.			
The nursing home has run the same ad for more than 3 weeks.			

How to Select a Nursing Home for a Loved One

Additional Comments:

Appendix B

Nursing Home Resident Rights

Nursing home residents have patient rights and certain protections under the law. The federal Nursing Home Reform Amendments of 1987, and corresponding state laws, protect residents in nearly all nursing facilities. This law requires that nursing facilities "promote and protect the rights of each resident." The resident's rights must be displayed in the nursing facility along with a contact number for the state's Long Term Care Ombudsman.

General goals of the law

The general goals of the Nursing Home Reform Amendments law are four-fold:

1) Quality of life
2) Provision of services and activities
3) Participation in facility administration
4) Access to the Ombudsman Program

Quality of life

The law requires nursing homes to "care for the residents in such a manner and in such an environment as will promote maintenance or enhancement of the quality of life of each resident." A new emphasis is placed on dignity, choice, and self-determination for nursing home residents.

Provision of services and activities

The law requires each nursing home to provide services and activities to attain or maintain the highest practicable physical, mental, and psychosocial well-being of each resident in accordance with a written plan of care that is initially prepared, with participation to the extent practicable of the resident or the resident's legal representative.

Participation in home administration

The law makes "resident and advocate participation" part of the criteria for assessing a home's compliance with administration requirements

Access to the Ombudsman Program

The law grants immediate access by ombudsmen to residents and reasonable access, in accordance with state law, by ombudsmen to records; requires homes to inform residents how to get in touch with ombudsmen to voice complaints, or in the event of a transfer or discharge from the home; requires state agencies to share inspection results with ombudsmen. Your contact with the ombudsmen is confidential.

Specific Resident Rights

Rights To Self-Determination

Nursing home residents have the rights to:
1) Choose their personal physician.
2) Get full information, in advance, and participate in planning and making any changes in their care and treatment.
3) Reside and receive services with reasonable accommodation by the home of individual needs and preferences.
4) Voice grievances about care or treatment they do or do not receive without discrimination or reprisal, and to receive prompt response from the home.
5) Organize and participate in resident groups (and their families have the right to organize family groups) in the home.

Personal and Privacy Rights
Nursing home residents have the rights to:

1) Participation in social, religious, and community activities as they choose.
2) Privacy in medical treatment, accommodations, personal visits, written and telephone conversations and meetings of resident and family groups.
3) Confidentiality of personal and clinical records.

Rights regarding abuse and restraints

Nursing home residents have the rights to:
1) Be free from physical or mental abuse, corporal punishment, involuntary seclusion, or disciplinary use of restraints;
2) Be free of restraints used for the convenience of the staff rather than the well-being of the residents;
3) Have restraints used only under written physician's orders to treat a resident's medical symptoms and to ensure the resident's safety and the safety of others; and
4) Be given psychopharmacologic medication only as ordered by a physician as a part of a written plan of care for a specific medical symptom, with annual review for appropriateness by an independent, external expert

Rights to information:
Nursing homes must:
1) Upon request provide residents with the latest inspection results and any plan of correction submitted by the home;
2) Notify residents in advance of any plans to change their rooms or roommate;
3) Inform residents of their rights upon admission and provide a written copy of the rights, including their rights regarding personal funds and their right to file a complaint with the state survey agency;
4) Inform residents in writing, at admission and throughout their stay, of the services available under the basic rate and of any extra charges for extra services, including, for Medicaid residents, a list of services covered by Medicaid

and those for which there is an extra charge; and
5) Prominently display and provide oral and written information for residents about how to apply for and use Medicaid benefits and how to receive a refund for previous private payments that Medicaid will pay retroactively

Right to visits
The nursing home must:

1) Permit immediate visits by a resident's personal physician and by representatives from the licensing agency and the Ombudsman Program.
2) Permit immediate visits by a resident's relatives, with the resident's consent.
3) Permit visits "subject to reasonable restriction" for others who visit with the resident's consent.
4) Permit ombudsmen to review resident's clinical records if a resident grants permission.

Transfer and discharge rights

Nursing homes "must permit each resident to remain in the facility and must not transfer or discharge the resident unless":
1) The transfer or discharge is necessary to meet the resident's welfare because the home cannot do so.
2) The transfer or discharge is appropriate because the resident's health has improved such that the resident no longer needs nursing home care.
3) The health or safety of other residents is endangered.

4) The resident has failed, after reasonable notice, to pay an allowable facility charge for an item or service provided upon the resident's request.
5) The home ceases to operate.
6) Residents and their representatives must be notified of a transfer at least 30 days in advance, or as soon as possible if more immediate changes in health require more immediate transfer.

In addition, the resident must be told:
1) The reason for the transfer.
2) His or her right to appeal the transfer.
3) The name, address, and phone number of the Ombudsman Program and protection and advocacy programs for the mentally ill and developmentally disabled.
4) Their right to request that their bed be held, including information about how many days Medicaid will pay for the bed to be held and the facility's bed-hold policies, and the right to return to the next available bed if Medicaid bed-holding coverage lapses.
5) A home must also prepare and orient residents to ensure a safe and orderly transfer or discharge.

Protection of personal funds

A nursing home must not require residents to deposit their personal funds with the home. If it does accept written responsibility for a resident's funds, **the nursing home must:**

1) Keep funds totaling more than $50 in an interest-bearing account, separate from the home's account.
2) Keep other funds available in a separate account or petty cash fund.
3) Keep a complete and separate accounting of each resident's funds, with a written record of all transactions, available for review by residents and their representatives.
4) Notify Medicaid residents when their balance account comes within $200 of the Medicaid limit and the effect of this on their eligibility.
5) Upon a resident's death, turn funds over to the resident's trustee.
6) Purchase a surety bond to secure residents' funds in its keeping.
7) Not charge a resident for any item or service covered by Medicaid, specifically including routine personal hygiene items and services.

Protection against Medicaid discrimination
Nursing homes must:
1) Establish and maintain identical policies and practices regarding transfer, discharge and the provision of services required under Medicaid for all individuals regardless of source of payment.
2) Not require residents to waive their rights to Medicaid, and must provide information about how to apply for Medicaid.

3) Not require a third party to guarantee payment as a condition of admission or continued stay; and
4) Not "charge, solicit, accept or receive" gifts, money, donations or "other consideration" as a precondition for admission or for continued stay by people eligible for Medicaid.

Appendix C

RESOURCES

OMBUDSMEN

Alabama

Virginia Moore-Bell
State LTC Ombudsman
AL Dept. of Senior Services 770 Washington Avenue
RSA Plaza, Suite 470
Montgomery, AL 36130
Tel: (334) 242-5743
Fax: (334) 242-5594
Website: http://www.alabamaageline.gov/ltc.cfm

Alaska
Robert Dreyer
State LTC Ombudsman
Office of the State LTC Ombudsman
AK Mental Health Trust Auth.
550 West 7th Avenue
Suite 1830
Anchorage, AK 99501
Tel: (907) 334-4480
Fax: (907) 334-4486
Website: http://www.akoltco.org

Arizona
Robert Nixon
State LTC Ombudsman
AZ Aging & Adult Administration
1789 West Jefferson
#950-A

Phoenix, AZ 85007
Tel: (602) 542-6454
Fax: (602) 542-6575
Website: https://www.azdes.gov/daas/ltco/

Arkansas
Kathie Gately
State LTC Ombudsman
AR Division of Aging & Adult Services
P.O.B. 1437
Slot S530
Little Rock, AR 72203-1437
Tel: (501) 682-8952
Fax: (501) 682-8155
Website: http://www.arombudsman.com/

California
Joe Rodrigues
State LTC Ombudsman
CA Department on Aging
1300 National Drive
Suite 200
Sacramento, CA 95834
Tel: (916) 419-7510
Fax: (916) 928-2503
Website: http://www.aging.ca.gov/Programs/LTCOP/

Colorado
Pat Tunnell
State LTC Ombudsman
The Legal Center
455 Sherman Street
Suite 130
Denver, CO 80203
Tel: (800) 288-1376

Fax: (303) 722-0720
Website: http://www.thelegalcenter.org/index.php?s=10298

Connecticut
Maggie Ewald
Acting State LTC Ombudsman
Office of the State LTC Ombudsman
CT Department of Social Services
25 Sigourney Street
12th Floor
Hartford, CT 06106-5033
Tel: (860) 424-5200
Fax: (860) 424-4808
Website: http://www.ltcop.state.ct.us/

Delaware
Beverly Morris
Acting State LTC Ombudsman
Division of Services for Aging & Adults
1901 North Dupont Highway
Main Admin. Bldg. Annex
New Castle, DE 19720
Tel: (302) 255-9390
Fax: (302) 255-4445
Website: http://dhss.delaware.gov/dhss/main/ltcop.html

District of Columbia
Gerald Kasunic
State LTC Ombudsman
Legal Counsel for the Elderly
601 E Street, N.W.
Washington, DC 20049
Tel: (202) 434-2140
Fax: (202) 434-6595 Website:
http://www.aarp.org/states/dc/LCE.html

Florida
Brian Lee
State LTC Ombudsman
Department of Elder Affairs
Florida State LTC Ombudsman Council
4040 Esplanade Way
Tallahassee, FL 32399
Tel: (888) 831-0404
Fax: (850) 414-2377
Website: http://ombudsman.myflorida.com/

Georgia
Becky Kurtz
State LTC Ombudsman
Office of the State LTCO
2 Peachtree Street, NW
9th Floor
Atlanta, GA 30303-3142
Tel: (888) 454-5826
Fax: (404) 463-8384
Website: http://www.georgiaombudsman.org

Hawaii
John McDermott
State LTC Ombudsman
Executive Office on Aging
250 South Hotel Street
Suite 406
Honolulu, HI 96813-2831
Tel: (808) 586-0100
Fax: (808) 586-0185
Website: http://hawaii.gov/health/eoa/LTCO.html

Idaho
Cathy Hart
State LTC Ombudsman
Idaho Commission on Aging
P.O. Box 83720
3380 American Terrace, Suite 120
Boise, ID 83720-0007
Tel: (208) 334-3833
Fax: (208) 334-3033
Website:
http://www.idahoaging.com/ombudsman/index.html

Illinois
Sally Petrone
State LTC Ombudsman
Illinois Department on Aging
421 East Capitol Avenue
Suite 100
Springfield, IL 62701-1789
Tel: (217) 785-3143
Fax: (217) 524-9644
Website: http://www.state.il.us/aging

Iowa
Jeanne Yordi
State LTC Ombudsman
Iowa Department of Elder Affairs
Clemens Building
200 10th Street, 3rd Floor
Des Moines, IA 50309-3609
Tel: (515) 242-3327
Fax: (515) 242-3300
Website:
http://www.aging.iowa.gov/advocacy/ombudsman.html

How to Select a Nursing Home for a Loved One

Indiana
Arlene Franklin
State LTC Ombudsman
Indiana Division Disabilities\Rehab Services
402 W. Washington St., Room W 454
PO Box 7083, MS21
Indianapolis, IN 46207-7083
Tel: (800) 545-7763
Fax: (317) 232-7867
Website: http://www.in.gov/fssa/da/3474.htm

Kansas
Kathy Greenlee
State LTC Ombudsman
Office of the State LTC Ombudsman
900 SW Jackson Street
Suite 1041
Topeka, KS 66612
Tel: (785) 296-3017
Fax: (785) 296-3916
Website: http://www.kansasombudsmanksgov.com/

Kentucky
Charles Smith
State LTC Ombudsman
Office of the Ombudsman
Cabinet for Health & Family Services
275 East Main Street
1E-B
Frankfort, KY 40621
Tel: (502) 564-5497
Fax: (502) 564-9523
Website: http://cfc.ky.gov/agencies/Ombudsman/

Louisiana
Linda Sadden
State LTC Ombudsman
Office of Elderly Affairs
412 N. 4th Street, 3rd Floor
P.O. Box 61
Baton Rouge, LA 70821
Tel: (225) 342-6872
Fax: (225) 342-7144
Website:
http://wwwprd.doa.louisiana.gov/laservices/publicpages/Se
rviceDetail.cfm?service_id=2803

Maine
Brenda Gallant
State LTC Ombudsman
Maine LTC Ombudsman Program
1 Weston Court
P.O. Box 128
Augusta, ME 04332
Tel: (207) 621-1079
Fax: (207) 621-0509
Website: http://www.maineombudsman.org

Maryland
Patricia Bayliss
State LTC Ombudsman
Maryland Department of Aging
301 W. Preston Street
Room 1007
Baltimore, MD 21201
Tel: (410) 767-1091
Fax: (410) 333-7943
Website: http://www.aging.maryland.gov/senior.html

Massachusetts
Mary McKenna
State LTC Ombudsman
State LTC Ombudsman
Massachusetts Exec Office of Elder Affairs
1 Ashburton Place
5th Floor
Boston, MA 02108-1518
Tel: (617) 727-7750
Fax: (617) 727-9368
Website: http://www.mass.gov/elders/service-orgs-advocates/ltc-ombudsman/ltc-ombudsman-overview.html

Michigan
Sarah Slocum
State LTC Ombudsman
Michigan Office of Services to the Aging
7109 West Saginaw
P.O. Box 30676
Lansing, MI 48909
Tel: (517) 335-0148
Fax: (517) 373-4092
Website: http://www.michigan.gov/miseniors/0,4635,7-234-49992-191521--,00.html

Minnesota
Jean Wood
Acting State LTC Ombudsman
Office of Ombudsman for Older Minnesotans
121 East Seventh Place
Suite 410
St. Paul, MN 55101
Tel: (651) 296-0382
Fax: (651) 297-5654
Website: http://www.mnaging.org.

Mississippi
Anniece McLemore
State LTC Ombudsman
State LTC Ombudsman
MS Dept. of Human Services, Div. of Aging
750 North State Street
Jackson, MS 39202
Tel: (601) 359-4927
Fax: (601) 359-9664
Website: http://www.mdhs.state.ms.us

Missouri
Carol Scott
State LTC Ombudsman
Department of Health & Senior Services
P.O. Box 570
Jefferson City, MO 65102
Tel: (800) 309-3282
Fax: (573) 526-4314
Website: http://health.mo.gov/seniors/ombudsman/

Montana
Kelly Moorse
State LTC Ombudsman
MT Dept. of Health & Human Services
P.O. Box 4210
111 N. Sanders
Helena, MT 59604-4210
Tel: (800) 551-3191
Fax: (406) 444-7743
Website:
http://www.dphhs.mt.gov/sltc/services/aging/ltcombudsman.shtml

Nebraska
Cindy Kadavy
State LTC Ombudsman
Division of Aging Services
P.O. Box 95044
Lincoln, NE 68509-5044
Tel: (402) 471-2307
Fax: (402) 471-4619
Website:
http://dhhs.ne.gov/medicaid/Pages/ags_ltcombud.aspx

Nevada
Kay Panelli
State Long-Term Care Ombudsman
Nevada Division for Aging Services
445 Apple Street
Suite 104
Reno, NV 89502
Tel: (775) 688-2964
Fax: (775) 688-2969
Website: http://www.nvaging.net/ltc.htm

New Hampshire
Don Rabun
State LTC Ombudsman
NH LTC Ombudsman Program
129 Pleasant Street
Concord, NH 03301-3857
Tel: (603) 271-4704
Fax: (603) 271-5574
Website: http://www.dhhs.nh.gov/oltco/index.htm

New Jersey
William Isele
State LTC Ombudsman

Office of Ombudsman for Institutional Elderly
P.O. Box 807
Trenton, NJ 08625-0807
Tel: (609) 943-4026
Fax: (609) 943-3479
Website: http://www.nj.gov/ooie/

New Mexico
Walter Lombardi
State LTC Ombudsman
New Mexico Aging & LTC Services Dept.
1015 Tijeras Avenue, N.W.
Suite 200
Albuquerque, NM 87102
Tel: (505) 222-4500
Fax: (505) 222-4526

New York
Martha Haase
State LTC Ombudsman
New York State Office for the Aging
2 Empire State Plaza
Agency Building #2
Albany, NY 12223
Tel: (518) 474-7329
Fax: (518) 474-7761
Website: http://www.ltcombudsman.ny.gov/

North Carolina
Sharon Wilder
State LTC Ombudsman
NC Division of Aging & Adult Services
2101 Mail Service Center
Raleigh, NC 27699-2101
Tel: (919) 733-8395

Fax: (919) 715-0868
Website: http://www.dhhs.state.nc.us/aging/ombud.htm

North Dakota
Helen Funk
State LTC Ombudsman
Long Term Care Ombudsman Prog.
Aging Services Division
600 E. Boulevard Avenue
Dept. 325
Bismarck, ND 58505
Tel: (800) 451-8693
Fax: (701) 328-4061
Website:
http://www.nd.gov/dhs/services/adultsaging/ombudsman.html

Ohio
Beverley Laubert
State LTC Ombudsman
Ohio Department of Aging
50 W Broad Street
9th Floor
Columbus, OH 43215-3363
Tel: (614) 466-1221
Fax: (614) 644-5201
Website: http://www.goldenbuckeye.com

Oklahoma
Esther Houser
State LTC Ombudsman
Long Term Care Ombudsman Prog.
DHS Aging Services Division
2401 N.W. 23rd Street
Suite 40
Oklahoma City, OK 73107

Tel: (405) 521-6734
Fax: (405) 522-6739
Website:
http://www.okdhs.org/divisionsoffices/visd/asd/ltc/

Oregon
Meredith Cote
State LTC Ombudsman
Oregon Office of the LTC Ombudsman
3855 Wolverine NE
Suite 6
Salem, OR 97305-1251
Tel: (503) 378-6533
Fax: (503) 373-0852
Website: http://www.oregon.gov/ltco/index.shtml

Pennsylvania
Wilmarie Gonzalez
State LTC Ombudsman
Pennsylvania Department of Aging
555 Walnut Street, 5th Floor
P.O. Box 1089
Harrisburg, PA 17101
Tel: (717) 783-1550
Fax: (717) 772-3382
Website:
http://www.portal.state.pa.us/portal/server.pt/community/advocacy_(ombudsman)/19389

Rhode Island
Roberta Hawkins
State LTC Ombudsman
Alliance for Better Long Term Care
422 Post Road
Suite 204

Warwick, RI 02888
Tel: (401) 785-3340
Fax: (401) 785-3391
Website:
http://adrc.ohhs.ri.gov/livingathome/long_term.php

South Carolina
Jon Cook
State LTC Ombudsman
SC DHHS, Office on Aging
1301 Gervais Street
Suite 200
Columbia, SC 29201
Tel: (803) 734-9900
Fax: (803) 734-9886
Website:
http://aging.sc.gov/seniors/ombudsman/Pages/index.aspx

South Dakota
Jeff Askew
State LTC Ombudsman
Department of Social Services
SD Office of Adult Services & Aging
700 Governors Drive
Pierre, SD 57501-2291
Tel: (605) 773-3656
Fax: (605) 773-6834
Website:
www.state.sd.us/social/ASA/services/ombudsman.htm

Tennessee
Adrian Wheeler
State LTC Ombudsman
TN Commission on Aging and Disability
Andrew Jackson Bldg.

500 Deaderick Street, Ste. 825
Nashville, TN 37243
Tel: (615) 741-2056
Fax: (615) 741-3309
Website:
http://www.state.tn.us/comaging/ombudsman.html

Texas
John Willis
State LTC Ombudsman
State Long Term Care Ombudsman Prog.
Texas Department of Aging and Disability Serv
701 West 51st Street
P.O. Box 149030, Mail Code: 250
Austin, TX 78714-9030
Tel: (512) 438-4356
Fax: (512) 438-4374
Website:
http://www.dads.state.tx.us/news_info/ombudsman/

Utah
Chad McNiven
State LTC Ombudsman
Department of Human Services
Utah Division of Aging & Adult Services
120 North 200 West
Room 325
Salt Lake City, UT 84103
Tel: (801) 538-3910
Fax: (801) 538-4395
Website: http://daas.utah.gov/ombudsman/index.html

Vermont
Jacqueline Majoros
State LTC Ombudsman

Vermont Legal Aid, Inc.
264 N. Winooski Avenue
P.O. Box 1367
Burlington, VT 05402
Tel: (802) 863-5620
Fax: (802) 863-7152
Website: http://www.vtlegalaid.org/our-projects/vermont-long-term-care-ombudsman/

Virginia
Joani Latimer
State LTC Ombudsman
VA Association of Area Agencies on Aging
24 E. Cary Street
Suite 100
Richmond, VA 23219
Tel: (804) 565-1600
Fax: (804) 644-5640
Website: http://www.vaaaa.org

Washington
Kary Hyre
State LTC Ombudsman
Multi-Service Center
1200 South 336th Street
P.O. Box 23699
Federal Way, WA 98093
Tel: (800) 422-1384
Fax: (253) 815-8173
Website: http://www.ltcop.org/index.htm

West Virginia
Larry Medley
State LTC Ombudsman
West Virginia Bureau of Senior Services

1900 Kanawha Boulevard East
Bldg #10
Charleston, WV 25305-0160
Tel: (304) 558-3317
Fax: (304) 558-0004
Website: http://www.state.wv.us/seniorservices/

Wisconsin
George Potaracke
State LTC Ombudsman
Wisconsin Board on Aging & Long Term Care
1402 Pankratz Street
Madison, WI 53704-4001
Tel: (800) 815-0015
Fax: (608) 246-7001
Website:
http://www.dhs.wisconsin.gov/aging/boaltc/ltcombud.htm

Wyoming
Deborah Alden
State LTC Ombudsman
Wyoming Senior Citizens, Inc
756 Gilchrist, P.O. Box 94
Wheatland, WY 82201
Tel: (307) 322-5553
Fax: (307) 322-3283
Website: http://www.wyomingseniors.com/services/long-term-care-ombudsman

Guam
Evelyn Cruz
State LTC Ombudsman
Division of Senior Citizens, Guam DPHSS
P.O. Box 2816
Hagatna, GU 96932

Tel: (671) 735-7382
Fax: (671) 735-7416
Website: http://dphss.guam.gov/content/long-term-care-ombudsman-services-program

Puerto Rico
Carmen Matos
State LTC Ombudsman
Puerto Rico Governor's Office of Elder Affairs
Call Box 50063
Old San Juan Station
San Juan, PR 00902
Tel: (787) 725-1515
Fax: (787) 721-6510

CITIZEN GROUPS

Alabama
Alabama Advocates for Quality Care
3717 Midway Road
Adamsville, AL 35005
Contact: Dixie Kuykendall
ph: (205) 674-9853
e-mail: dixiek@charter.net

Arkansas
AR Advocates for Nursing Home Residents
961 Paul Drive
Conway, AR 72034
Contact: Nancy Allison
ph: (501) 327-3152
fax: (501) 884-6728
e-mail: info@aanhr.org
Website: http://www.aanhr.org

AR Advocates for Nursing Home Residents

P.O. Box 22421
Little Rock, AR 72221-2421
Contact: Virginia Cross
ph: (501) 225-4082
fax: (501) 884-6728
e-mail: info@aanhr.org
Website: http://www.aanhr.org

AR Advocates for Nursing Home Residents
135 Hillview Drive
Apt 112
Fairfield Bay, AR 72088
Contact: Nancy Johnson
ph: (501) 884-6728
fax: (501) 884-6728
e-mail: info@aanhr.org
Website: http://www.aanhr.org

California
Foundation Aiding the Elderly
P.O. Box 254849
Sacramento, CA 95865-4849
Contact: Carole Herman
ph: (916) 481-8558
fax: (916) 481-8329
e-mail: carole@4fate.org
Website: http://www.4fate.org

CA Advocates for Nursing Home Reform
650 Harrison Street
2nd Floor
San Francisco, CA 94107-1311
Contact: Patricia McGinnis
ph: (415) 974-5171
fax: (415) 777-2904

e-mail: PatM@canhr.org
Website: http://www.canhr.org

Connecticut
CT Citizens Coalition for NH Reform
211 State Street
Bridgeport, CT 06604
Contact: Steven Kilpatrick
ph: (203) 336-3851
fax: (203) 333-4976
e-mail: skilpatrick@connlegalservices.org

Advocates for Loved Ones in Nursing Homes
28 B Damon Heights Road
Niantic, CT 06357
Contact: Maryann Lidestri
e-mail: aflon@hotmail.com

Florida
Fighting Elder Abuse Together (FEAT)
1625 La Maderia Dr., S.W.
Palm Bay, FL 32908
Contact: Judy Ahler-Friddle
ph: (321) 984-8883
fax: (321) 956-7606
e-mail: ahler_friddle@msn.com
Coalition to Protect America's Elders
3699 Plowshare Road
Tallahassee, FL 32309
Contact: Barbara Hengstebeck
ph: (850) 216-2727
fax: (850) 216-1933
e-mail: coalitiontoprotect@comcast.net
Website: http://www.protectelders.org

Quality Care Advocates, Inc
P.O. Box 494224
Port Charlotte, FL 33949
Contact: Linda Pounds
ph: (941) 743-0987
e-mail: llpsterling@aol.com

Advocates Committed To Improving Our NH's
4714 W. Euclid Ave.
Tampa, FL 33629
Contact: Anna Spinella
ph: (813) 837-1714
e-mail: amspinel@tampabay.rr.com

Georgia
Georgia Council on Aging
2 Peachtree Street, NW
Suite 32-270
Atlanta, GA 30303
Contact: Melanie McNeil
ph: (404) 657-5348
fax: (404) 657-1722
e-mail: msmcneil@dhr.state.ga.us
Website: http://www.gcoa.org

Illinois
Nursing Home Monitors
6111 Vollmer Lane
Godfrey, IL 62035
Contact: Violette King
ph: (618) 466-3410
fax: (618) 466-3410
e-mail: vkmonitor@earthlink.net
Website: http://www.nursinghomemonitors.org

Illinois Citizens For Better Care
220 South State Street
Suite 1928
Chicago, IL 60604
Contact: Wendy Meltzer
ph: (312) 663-5120
fax: (312) 427-0181
e-mail: wmicbc@core.com

Tender Loving Care in Long Term Care
620 North Walnut St.
Springfield, IL 62702
Contact: Margaret Niederer
ph: (217) 523-8488
fax: (217) 523-8493
e-mail: email@tlcinltc.org

Indiana
United Senior Action
324 W. Morris Street
Suite 114
Indianapolis, IN 46225-1491
Contact: Robyn Grant
ph: (317) 634-0872
fax: (317) 687-3661
e-mail: robyngrant@comcast.net

Kansas
Kansas Advocates for Better Care
913 Tennessee Street, #2
Lawrence, KS 66044
Contact: Deanne Bacco
ph: (800) 525-1782
fax: (785) 749-0029

e-mail: info@kabc.org
Website: http://www.kabc.org

Kentucky
Kentuckians for Nursing Home Reform
1530 Nicholasville Road
Lexington, KY 40503
Contact: Bernie Vonderheide
ph: (859) 312-5617
e-mail: kynursinghomereform@yahoo.com
Website: http://www.kynursinghomereform.org

Louisiana
Citizens Care
1321 8th Street
New Orleans, LA 70118
Contact: Doris Taylor
ph: (504) 896-8912
e-mail: citizens@citizenscare.org

Maryland
Voices for Quality Care (LTC)
PO Box 6555, US Postal Service
St. Charles Town Center Mall
Waldorf, MD 20603
Contact: Kate Ricks
ph: (888) 600-2375
e-mail: voicesforqualitycare@hotmail.com
Website: http://www.voicesforqualitycare.org

Massachusetts
MA Advocates for Nursing Home Reform
38 Banks Terrace
Swampscott, MA 01907
Contact: Arlene Germain

ph: (781) 890-2244
fax: (781) 890-4956
e-mail: agermain@matrixpartners.com
Website: http://www.manhr.org

Cape United Elders of Comm. Action Committee
115 Enterprise Road
Hyannis, MA 02601
Contact: Susan Walker
ph: (508) 771-1727
fax: (508) 775-7488
e-mail: susanw@cacci.cc

Michigan
Michigan Campaign for Quality Care
5886 Highgate Avenue
East Lansing, MI 48823
Contact: Alison Hirschel
ph: (517) 324-5754
fax: (517) 333-4339
e-mail: hirschel@umich.edu
Website: http://www.campaignforqualitycare.org
Citizens For Better Care
4750 Woodward Avenue
Suite 410
Detroit, MI 48201-1308
Contact: Nancy Jackson
ph: (313) 832-6387
fax: (313) 832-7407
e-mail: cbcnancyj@yahoo.com
Website: http://cbcmi.org

Minnesota
ElderCare Rights Alliance
2626 East 82nd Street

Suite 230
Bloomington, MN 55425
Contact: Tom Hyder
ph: (952) 854-7304
fax: (952) 854-8535
e-mail: thyder@eldercarerights.org

Missouri
Missouri Coalition for Quality Care
P.O. Box 7165
Jefferson City, MO 65102
Contact: Georgia Sanders
ph: (888) 262-5644
e-mail: mail@mcqc.com
Website: http://www.mcqc.com

Nebraska
Nebraska Advocates for Nursing Home Residents
10050 Regency Circle
Suite 525
Omaha, NE 68114
Contact: Bill Seidler
ph: (402) 397-3801
fax: (402) 397-3869
e-mail: bjseidler@qwest.net

New Mexico
New Mexicans for Quality Long Term Care
P.O. Box 1712
Belen, NM 87002
Contact: J.C. Beverly
ph: (505) 864-7534
fax: (505) 864-7377
e-mail: jcbeverly@msn.com

New York
Coalition of Institutionalized Aged and Disab
425 East 25th Street
New York, NY 10010
Contact: Geoff Lieberman
ph: (212) 481-7572
fax: (212) 481-5149
e-mail: ciadny@aol.com
Website: http://www.ciadny.org

Long Term Care Community Coalition
242 West 30th Street
Suite 306
New York, NY 10001
Contact: Richard Mollot
ph: (212) 385-0355
fax: (212) 239-2801
e-mail: richard@ltccc.org
Website: http://www.ltccc.org

FRIA
18 John Street
Suite 905
New York, NY 10038
Contact: Amy Paul
ph: (212) 732-5667
fax: (212) 732-6945
e-mail: apaul@fria.org
Website: http://www.fria.org/fria/

North Carolina
Friends of Residents In Long Term Care
883-C Washington St.
Raleigh, NC 27605
Contact: Bill Lamb
ph: (919) 782-1530

fax: (919) 782-1558
e-mail: friends@forltc.org
Website: http://www.forltc.org/cms/

Ohio
Families For Improved Care Inc.
P.O. Box 21398
Columbus, OH 43221-1355
Contact: Donald Greenberg
ph: (614) 459-8438
e-mail: fficgroup@aol.com

Oklahoma
Oklahomans for Improvement of NH Care
1423 Oakwood Drive
Norman, OK 73069-4446
Contact: JoAnna Deighton
ph: (405) 364-5004
fax: (405) 364-5004
e-mail: JADCD@aol.com

Pennsylvania
CARIE
100 N. 17th Street
Suite 600
Philadelphia, PA 19103
Contact: Diane Menio
ph: (215) 545-5728
fax: (215) 546-9963
e-mail: menio@carie.org
Website: http://www.carie.org

Rhode Island
Alliance for Better Long Term Care
422 Post Road

Suite 204
Warwick, RI 02888
Contact: Roberta Hawkins
ph: (401) 785-3340
fax: (401) 785-3391
e-mail: rhawkins@alliancebltc.org
Website: http://www.alliancebltc.com/page14.php

Texas
Texas Advocates for Nursing Home Residents
500 East Anderson Ln.
#234W
Austin, TX 78752
Contact: Beth Ferris
ph: (512) 719-4757
fax: (512) 719-5057
e-mail: bethferris@peoplepc.com

Texas Advocates for Nursing Home Residents
1015 Wavecrest Dr.
Houston, TX 77062
Contact: Gay Nell Harper
ph: (281) 488-5291
fax: (281) 480-4351
e-mail: sealbeem@aol.com

Texas Advocates for Nursing Home Residents
634 Green Cove Lane
Dallas, TX 75232
Contact: Lou O'Reilly
ph: (972) 572-6330
fax: (214) 376-7707
e-mail: oreillyl@swbell.net
Texans For The Improvement of Long-Term Care
4545 Cook Road, #303

Houston, TX 77072-1125
Contact: Sam Perlin
ph: (281) 933-4533
fax: (281) 498-6344
e-mail: sperlin@aol.com

Virginia
Citizens Committee to Protect the Elderly
407 Oakmears Crescent
Virginia Beach, VA 23462
Contact: Judith Allison
 ph: (757) 518-8500
fax: (757) 518-8501
e-mail: citizenscommittee@citizenscommittee.org
Website: http://www.citizenscommittee.org/

TLC for Long Term Care
P.O. Box 523323
Springfield, VA 22152
Contact: Dale Belrose
ph: (703) 338-7333
fax: (866) 487-8470
e-mail: tlc4ltc@msn.com

Virginia Friends & Relatives of NH Residents
1426 Claremount Avenue
Richmond, VA 23227
Contact: Joani Latimer
ph: (804) 644-2804
fax: (804) 644-5640
e-mail: elderights@aol.com
Friends & Relatives of Nursing Home Residents
P.O. Box 551
Harrisonburg, VA 22803
Contact: Anne Scott See

ph: (540) 896-2741
fax: (540) 433-2202
e-mail: asbrls@hotmail.com

Washington
Family Advocates for NH Improvement
10955 W. Villa Monte Drive
Mukilteo, WA 98275
Contact: Mary Gorale
ph: (888) 647-3367
fax: (888) 647-3367
e-mail: fanhimg@aol.com

Resident Councils of Washington
220 E. Canyon View Road
Belfair, WA 98528
Contact: Sharon McIntyre
ph: (360) 275-8000
fax: (360) 277-0144
e-mail: rcwexec@residentcouncil.org

Wyoming
Concerned Citizens For Quality Nsg Home Care
811 Glenn Road
Casper, WY 82601
Contact: Virginia King
ph: (307) 266-6659
e-mail: eca@wyoming.com

NURSING HOME ABUSE HOTLINES

Alabama
1-800-458-7214
More Information
Alabama Department of Senior Services

Alaska
1-800-730-6393 (Toll free in Alaska)
Outside of Alaska: 907-334-4483

Arizona
1-SOS-ADULT or 1-877-767-2385
602-674-4200
TDD: 1-877-815-8390

Arkansas
1-800-582-4887
In Pulaski County: (501) 682-8425
Fax: (501) 682-1967, Attention Complaint Unit
E-mail: complaints.OLTC@arkansas.gov
More Information
Arkansas Office of Long Term Care, Complaints Unit
Arkansas Long Term Care Ombudsman

California
1-800-231-4024
More Information
California Long Term Care Ombudsman

Colorado
1-800-773-1366 or

1-800-886-7689, Ext. 2800
(303) 692-2800
E-mail: health.facilities@state.co.us
Fax: (303) 753-6214
More Information
Colorado Department of Public Health Nursing Home Complaints Program
Connecticut

1-860-424-5241

Delaware
1-800-223-9074

District of Columbia
202-434-2140

Florida
1-800-96ABUSE or 1-800-962-2873

Georgia
1-800-878-6442
(404) 657-5728 (Metro-Atlanta)
More Information
Georgia Office of Regulatory Services

Guam
(671) 475-0268
After Hours: 671-646-4455
(evenings, weekends, holidays)

Hawaii
(808) 832-5115(Oahu)
(808) 243-5151 (Maui, Molokai, and Lanai)

(808) 241-3432 (Kauai)
(808) 933-8820 (East Hawaii)
(808) 327-6280 (West Hawaii)

More Information
Hawaii Long Term Care Ombudsman
(808) 586-0100

Idaho
1-877-471-2777

Illinois
1-800-252-4343 (Toll free in Illinois)
TTY: 1-800-547-0466
Outside of Illinois: 217-785-0321
More Information
Illinois Department on Aging

Indiana
1-800-992-6978 (Toll free in Indiana)
Outside of Indiana: 1-800-545-7763, Ext. 20135

Iowa
1-800-686-0027 or
1-877-686-0027
More Information
Iowa Long Term Care Ombudsman

Iowa Department of Inspections and Appeals, Health Facilities Division

Kansas
1-800-842-0078
1-877-662-8362 (Toll free in Kansas)

Outside of Kansas: 785-296-3017
More Information
Kansas Office of the State Long Term Care Ombudsman

Kentucky
Elder Abuse Hotline: 1-800-752-6200
Long Term Care Ombudsman: 1-800-372-2991
TTY (for hearing impaired): 1-800-627-4702

Attorney General's Patient Abuse Tip Line: 1-877-ABUSE TIP (1-877-228-7384)

More Information
Office of the Attorney General Medicaid Fraud & Abuse Control Division
Kentucky Office of Inspector General

Louisiana
1-800-259-4990 (Toll free in Louisiana)
Outside of Louisiana: (225) 342-9722
Adults With Disabilities (Ages 18-59)
1-800-898-4910

Maine
1-800-383-2441 (Toll free in Maine)
Local/Out-of-State TTY: (207) 287-9312
More Information
Maine Department of Health and Human Services
Maryland
1-800-917-7383 (Toll free in Maryland)
1-800-AGE-DIAL, Ext. 1091 (Toll free in Maryland)
Outside of Maryland: (410) 767-1091
More Information
Maryland Long Term Care Ombudsman

Massachusetts
1-800-462-5540
1-800-AGE-INFO (1-800-243-4636)
Massachusetts Attorney General's Elder Hotline: 1-888-AG-ELDER
(1-888-243-5337)
TTY: (617) 727-0434

Michigan
1-800-882-6006
More Information
Michigan Bureau of Health Systems

Minnesota
1-800-333-2433
TDD/TYY: 1-800-627-3529

Mississippi
1-800-227-7308
1-800-222-8000 (Toll free in Mississippi)
Outside of Mississippi: (601) 359-4991

Missouri
1-800-392-0210

Montana
1-800-551-3191 (Toll free in Montana)
Outside of Montana: (406) 444-4077
More Information
Montana Senior & Long Term Care Division Ombudsman

Nebraska
1-800-652-1999 (Toll free in Nebraska)
Outside of Nebraska: (402) 595-1324

Nevada
1-800-992-5757 (Toll free in Nevada)
Outside of Nevada:
Carson City area: (775) 687-4210
Reno area: (775) 688-2964
Elko area: (775) 738-1966
Las Vegas area: (702) 486-3545

New Hampshire
1-800-442-5640 or
(603) 271-4375
More Information
New Hampshire Office of the Long Term Care Ombudsman

New Jersey
1-800-792-8820 (Toll free in New Jersey)
Outside of New Jersey: (609) 943-3473
E-mail: acs@doh.state.nj.us

New Mexico
1-800-797-3260 or
(505) 841-6100 (In Albuquerque)

New York
NURSING HOME COMPLAINTS
1-888-201-4563
E-Mail: nhintake@health.state.ny.us
ADULT CARE HOME COMPLAINTS
(866) 893-6772

More Information

New York State Department of Health

Nursing Homes
Adult Care Facilities

North Carolina
1-800-662-7030

North Dakota
1-800-451-8693

Ohio
1-800-342-0533
TDD: (614) 752-6490
Fax: (614) 728-9169
E-mail: HCComplaints@gw.odh.state.oh.us
More Information
Ohio Department of Health

Oklahoma
1-800-522-3511

Oregon
1-800-522-2602 or
(503) 378-6533
AGING/DEVELOPMENTAL DISABILITIES
1-800-866-406-4287 or
(503) 945-9495

More Information
Oregon Long Term Care Ombudsman
Oregon Department of Human Services Office of Investigations

Pennsylvania
1-800-254-5164
More Information
Pennsylvania Department of Health

Rhode Island
(401) 785-3340
Fax: (401) 785-3391

South Carolina
(803) 898-2850

South Dakota
(605) 773-3656

Tennessee
1-888-APS-TENN or 1-888-277-8366

Texas
1-800-458-9858 (Toll free in Texas)
Outside of Texas: (512) 834-3784

Utah
1-800-371-7897 (Toll free in Utah)
Outside of Utah: (801) 264-7669
E-mail: vruesch@utah.gov

Vermont
1-800-564-1612
(802) 241-2345
Fax (802) 241-2358
More Information
APS Online Report Form
Vermont Department of Aging & Independent Living

Virginia
1-888-83-ADULT or 1-888-832-3858
Richmond area: (804) 371-0896

Washington
1-800-562-6078

West Virginia
1-800-352-6513

Wisconsin
1-800-815-0015 (Toll free in Wisconsin)
Outside of Wisconsin: (608) 246-7013
More Information
Wisconsin Long Term Care Ombudsman

Wyoming
(307) 777-6137 or (307) 777-7123

More information:
Wyoming Long Term Care Ombudsman

Appendix D
Nursing Home Pre-Admission Form

Your nursing home may have its own preadmission form. If not, you can look at the sample which follows to get an idea of what to expect.

Name:
_____
_____

Address:
_____
_____

City:_____
State: _____ Zip:_____

Telephone: ( ) _____ - _____

Emergency Contact:
_____
_____

Telephone: ( ) _____ - _____

Social Security Number: _____

Medicare Number: _____

Present   Living   Arrangements:
_____
_____

Reason: _____
_____

PERSONAL HISTORY

Birthdate: _____

Place of Birth: _____

Marital Status: _____

Education: _____

Occupation:
_____
_____

Spouse's Name (Living or Not):
_____

Religion: _____

Church: _____

Church Address:
_____
_____

Clergy Name: _____

Telephone: (   ) _____ - _____

How to Select a Nursing Home for a Loved One

MEDICAL CONTACTS

Physician
_____
_____

Phone: ( ) _____ - _____

Dentist:
_____
_____

Phone: ( ) _____ - _____

Optometrist
_____
_____

Phone: ( ) _____ - _____

Podiatrist
_____
_____

Phone: ( ) _____ - _____

Pharmacy
_____
_____

Phone: ( ) _____ - _____

Hospital:

Bradley M. Lakin

_____
_____

Phone: (　) _____ - _____

Health Insurance Company:
_____
_____

Policy Numbers:
_____
_____

Funeral Home:
_____
_____

Address:
_____
_____

Phone:(　) _____ - _____

How to Select a Nursing Home for a Loved One

HEALTH INFORMATION

History of Medical Problems:

_____
_____
_____
_____
_____
_____
_____
_____

History of Major Operations:

_____
_____
_____
_____
_____
_____
_____
_____

Other:

How to Select a Nursing Home for a Loved One

Medication	Dosage	Frequency	Reason Prescribed

SPECIAL NEEDS	Yes	No	Explanation
Hearing difficulties			
Vision difficulties			
Special diet			
Able to feed self			
Special dinnerware			
Swelling			
Bedsores			
Catheter			
Incontinence			
Wandering			
Insomnia			
Bathing			
Help dressing			
Help teeth brushing			

How to Select a Nursing Home for a Loved One

Uses oxygen			
Uses walker			
Uses wheelchair			
Uses lift chair			
Uses raised toilet seat			
Other:			

DOCUMENTATION

Is there a Living Will?

Yes ____ No ____

Is there a Durable Power of Attorney for Health Care?

Yes ____ No ____

If yes, who is responsible for decisions?

_____

Is there a Power of Attorney (for finances)?

Yes ____ No ____

If yes, who is responsible for decisions?

_____

CONTACT PERSONS

Please provide the following information about family members.

Name: _____
Spouse: _____

Relationship:

_____
_____

Phone: (Home) _____
        (Work) _____

Address:

How to Select a Nursing Home for a Loved One

_____
_____

City:_____

State: _____ Zip _____

Name: _____
Spouse:_____

Relationship:
_____
_____

Phone: (Home)_____
          (Work)_____

Address:
_____
_____

City:_____

State: _____ Zip _____

Name: _____
Spouse:_____

Relationship:
_____
_____

Bradley M. Lakin

Phone: (Home)_____
        (Work)_____

Address:
_____
_____

City:_____

State:_____ Zip _____

Name:_____
Spouse:_____

Relationship:
_____
_____

Phone: (Home)_____
        (Work)_____

Address:
_____
_____

City:_____

State:_____ Zip _____

Name:_____
Spouse:_____

Relationship:

How to Select a Nursing Home for a Loved One

_____
_____

Phone: (Home)_____
         (Work)_____

Address:

_____
_____

City:_____

State: _____ Zip _____

Name: _____
Spouse:_____

Relationship:
_____
_____

Phone: (Home)_____
         (Work)_____

Address:
_____
_____

City:_____

State: _____ Zip _____

Name: _____
Spouse:_____

Bradley M. Lakin

Relationship:
_____
_____

Phone: (Home)_____
        (Work)_____

Address:
_____
_____

City:_____

State:_____ Zip _____

Name: _____
Spouse:_____

Relationship:
_____
_____

Phone: (Home)_____
        (Work)_____

Address:
_____
_____

City:_____

State:_____ Zip _____

Name: _____
Spouse:_____

How to Select a Nursing Home for a Loved One

Relationship:
_____
_____

Phone: (Home)_____
           (Work)_____

Address:
_____
_____

City:_____

State: _____ Zip _____

Made in the USA
Charleston, SC
01 February 2014